Common Core L
Branches c

By C

Published by Gallopade International, Inc.
©Carole Marsh/Gallopade
Printed in the U.S.A. (Peachtree City, Georgia)

TABLE OF CONTENTS

G: Includes Graphic Organizer

GO: Graphic Organizer is also available 8½" x 11" online
download at www.gallopade.com/client/go
(numbers above correspond to the graphic organizer numbers online)

Separation of Powers

Read the text and answer the questions.

From 1781 to 1789, the 13 states joined together under the Articles of Confederation. The Articles of Confederation created a central government made of a "loose <u>union</u> of states" in which the central government had little authority over the individual states. The central government only consisted of a unicameral Congress. The Articles gave some powers to Congress, but the central government lacked a leader, and Congress could not collect taxes or enforce laws in all the states.

Congress quickly divided into federalists and antifederalists. Federalists wanted a stronger central (federal) government to better manage the union of states. However, the antifederalists worried that a strong central government would become too powerful over the states. The delegates of the Constitutional Convention, who met in 1787 to write a new Constitution, came to an agreement. They decided that the central government should be given more power, but also be divided into three branches of government.

To prevent the government from becoming too powerful, the new Constitution divided powers and responsibilities among three distinct branches of government. This separation of power includes the legislative branch to write the laws, the executive branch to carry out and enforce the laws, and finally, the judicial branch to interpret and apply the law in the courts. This separation of powers addressed the concerns of both federalists and antifederalists.

1. A. Define <u>union</u> as it is used in the text.
    B. Why was the government created by the Articles of Confederation considered a "loose union of states"?

2. Why did antifederalists oppose a strong central government?

3. Why was the government divided? Name the three branches.

4. What document established the separation of powers?

5. List three differences between the Articles of Confederation and the new Constitution.

6. How did the separation of powers address the concerns of antifederalists?

The Great Compromise

Read the text and answer the questions.

On July 16, 1787, the delegates to the Constitutional Convention were hard at work writing a new Constitution. However, the issue of states' representation in the legislative branch quickly became a hotly debated topic.

The Virginia Plan proposed a bicameral, or two-house, Congress. Each house would be based on proportional representation. This meant that the population of a state determined how many representatives and senators the state could have. This plan favored more populated states, while less-populated states would be at a disadvantage.

Smaller states feared that their congressional votes would always be outweighed by larger states. Thus, they introduced the New Jersey Plan, which called for a unicameral Congress, where each state was allowed one vote. The New Jersey Plan was ultimately rejected, and smaller states' delegates threatened to leave the Constitutional Convention.

The Great Compromise, which was proposed by Roger Sherman of Connecticut, blended the Virginia and New Jersey Plans. Congress would be made up of a Senate and a House of Representatives. Each state would have an equal number of senators, but the number of representatives in the House of Representatives would be based on a state's population.

. Use Latin prefixes to explain the differences between a unicameral and a bicameral congress. What is a tricameral congress?

. Make inferences from the text to write a definition of proportional representation.

. A. What were the two key differences between the plans as described by the text?
   B. How did the Great Compromise resolve these differences?

. Write a short argument from the perspective of either a large state or a small state. Tell which plan you prefer, why you think it is best, and why you oppose the other plan. Present your argument as a debate with your classmates. Discuss the results of the Great Compromise.

Federalist Quotes

Rewrite each quotation to complete the chart. Use the completed chart to answer the questions.

Federalist quotations	What each quotation means to me
"To all general purposes we have uniformly been one people each individual citizens everywhere enjoying the same national rights, privileges, and protection." — *Alexander Hamilton* *The Federalist Papers*	
"In my opinion, these three great [branches of government] should be forever separated, and so distributed as to serve as checks on each other." — *John Jay to Thomas Jefferson*	
"The accumulation of all powers, legislative, executive, and judiciary, in the same hands, whether of one, a few, or many, and whether hereditary, self-appointed, or elective, may justly be pronounced the very definition of tyranny." — *James Madison*	

1. What is the common theme shared by all three quotations?

2. Why does Alexander Hamilton support a strong central government?

3. What reasons does John Jay give for why the "branches of government" should be separated?

4. Under what circumstances does James Madison believe separation of powers is necessary?

5. Which two quotations express the most similar positions? What is the key point on which they agree?

Checks and Balances

Read the text and answer the questions.

The Constitution established three distinct branches of government and gave each branch its powers. However, the Constitution also limits the powers of the three branches. A system of checks and balances ensures no one branch of government is able to abuse its power or become too powerful. Each branch has responsibilities and authority, but actions are checked and approved by the other branches.

Checks and Balances Example

The legislative branch, Congress, introduces a bill. Representatives vote and a majority vote passes the bill. The bill then goes to the executive branch for approval.

The executive branch has the power to approve or veto the bill. If the president, for example, does not approve of the bill, the president may veto it and send it back to Congress.

If the president vetoes the bill, Congress can check the power of the president by overruling the executive veto with a two-thirds majority vote in both houses.

Once a bill becomes a law, the judicial branch is responsible for interpreting the laws. The judicial branch has the power of judicial review. This means that the judicial branch can determine whether or not a law is constitutional (legal). This may be the end of the law—or not. The legislative branch may introduce a new bill very similar to the one that was revoked by the judicial branch. The process would then start all over again.

. Explain the relationship between "separation of powers" and "checks and balances."

. The legislative branch has the power to pass laws.
   A. What can the executive branch do to check the legislative branch?
   B. What can the legislative branch do to check the executive branch?
   C. What can the judicial branch do to check the legislative branch?
   D. What can the legislative branch do to check the judicial branch?

Executive Branch

Read the text and answer the questions.

The executive branch of the U.S. government is outlined in Article II of the U.S. Constitution. The executive branch is responsible for carrying out and enforcing the laws.

The head of the executive branch is the president. The president has the power to sign or veto bills proposed by Congress. The president negotiates and signs treaties, and maintains diplomatic relations with other countries. The president is the Commander-in-Chief of the U.S. Armed Forces. The president also has the power to pardon people convicted of federal crimes.

The president appoints Cabinet leaders to assist with his or her duties. The Cabinet consists of individuals who lead federal agencies, such as the Departments of Labor, Education, Energy, Agriculture, Justice, and others. These men and women advise the president on issues concerning their agencies. Each agency is vitally important to running various areas of the government. For example, the Department of Agriculture is in charge of food safety, protecting natural resources, and supporting farmers.

The president is faced with many challenging decisions every day. The Executive Office of the President, or EOP, is made up of advisors who support the president. The president selects his or her advisory team and the White House chief of staff oversees those advisors.

The vice president takes the place of the president when the president is no longer able to carry out his or her duties. The vice president serves as the president of the Senate and casts the deciding vote when there is a tie in the Senate.

1. Write an appropriate headline for each paragraph.

2. Create a main idea graphic organizer to identify the responsibilities of the president.

3. In what ways are the Cabinet and the EOP similar?

4. Use inferences from the text to explain the relationship between the president and the many members of the executive branch.

Presidential Cabinet

Read the text and answer the questions.

President George Washington formed the first presidential Cabinet with only four advisors. Today, the vice president and 15 department heads make up the Cabinet. The president appoints the Cabinet members with congressional approval. Cabinet members are the heads of executive departments and advise the president. Article II, section 1 of the U.S. Constitution refers to Cabinet members as principal officers of the executive departments. They are ranked in order of presidential succession.

1. How is the presidential Cabinet selected?

2. How has the Cabinet changed since it was first formed?

Use an online resource to complete the Cabinet chart in order of presidential succession.

President:
Vice President:

Departments	Department Heads

Roles of the President

Analyze the graphical organizer and complete the activity.

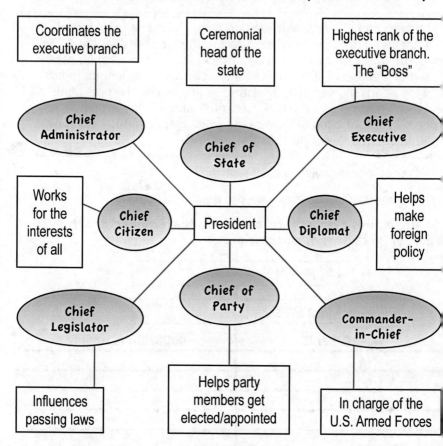

Use the graphic organizer to write at least two generalizations* about each of the following topics. Then cite evidence from the graphic organizer to support each generalization.

1. The importance of the president
2. What it would be like to be president
3. What skills you would need to be the president

Generalizations are broad statements or conclusions based on the review of many facts and details.

The Big Three

This photograph depicts the USSR leader Joseph Stalin, U.S. President Franklin D. Roosevelt, and Prime Minister of England Winston Churchill. These leaders of the Allies of WWII were known as "The Big Three."

Look at the photograph and answer the questions.

1. Make an inference about when this photograph was taken based on details in the photograph. Explain.

2. What can you infer about the person who took this photograph based on the position / order of the three leaders? Explain.

3. Compare and contrast the personalities presented by the leaders.

4. Predict what might be different had this picture been taken today.

5. Describe the roles of the president depicted in the photograph.

6. Create an Inference Ladder Graphic Organizer based on the leaders' attire (clothing), posture, and physical expressions.

Legislative Branch

Read the text and answer the questions.

The <u>legislative</u> branch of the United States government is outlined in Article I of the U.S. Constitution. A <u>bicameral</u> Congress, having two houses, makes up the U.S. legislative branch. Citizens of the United States elect all members of the legislative branch.

Congress is made up of the Senate and the House of Representatives. The Constitution gives Congress the exclusive power to make or change laws. Both houses are essential to the lawmaking process. To pass a law, both houses of Congress must pass a bill by a majority vote. If the president vetoes it, Congress can still pass the law with a two-thirds majority vote of both houses.

Each house of Congress has additional roles and responsibilities. The Senate has sole power to confirm or reject presidential appointments and ratify treaties. The House of Representatives has sole power to initiate tax bills, impeach federal officials, and elect the president if there is a tie in the Electoral College.

Congress holds other responsibilities as well, including the power to declare war and set the annual budget. This means that Congress can levy taxes and tariffs in order to pay for government services. Congress is responsible for deciding when and how to collect taxes and use taxpayer dollars.

1. A. Define <u>bicameral</u> as it is used in the text.
    B. List two additional words that have the same prefix.

2. From where does Congress get its power?

3. How are members of Congress selected?

4. A. Power to confirm or reject presidential appointments is an example of what two concepts established by the Constitution?
    B. What two branches are directly involved?

5. Create a main idea organizer to show the different functions of the legislative branch.

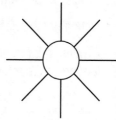

Roles and Responsibilities

Use an online resource to fill in the chart with the roles and responsibilities given to each house of Congress. Then answer the questions.

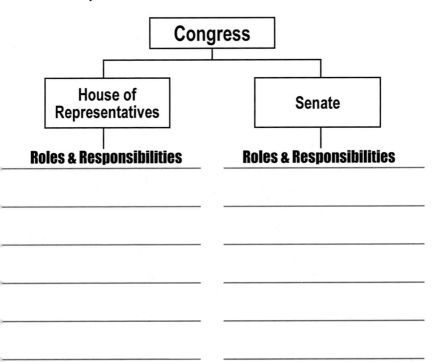

1. Describe the structure of the legislative branch.

2. According to your chart, which house of Congress has more responsibilities?

3. What can you infer about the relationship between the houses of Congress from their shared roles and responsibilities?

4. A. Use the chart to describe the legislative branch's role in the process of amending the Constitution.
   B. Use an online resource to research one of the amendments to the Constitution. Summarize the who, when, where, and why of the amendment in a short report. Proofread and edit your work.

Three Branches Flowchart

Complete the graphic organizer with information about the three branches of government.

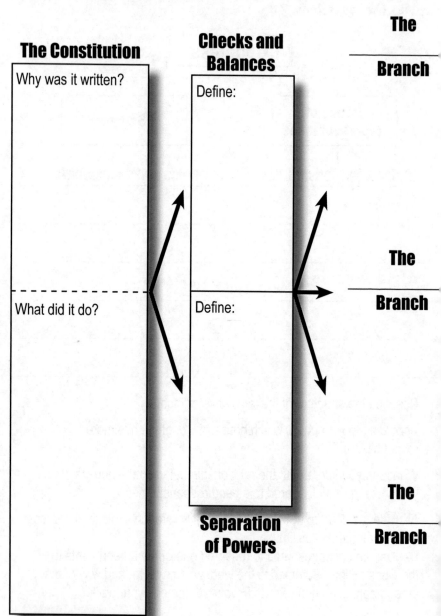

The Constitution

Why was it written?

What did it do?

Checks and Balances

Define:

Define:

Separation of Powers

The _____ Branch

The _____ Branch

The _____ Branch

Who? | Does What? | Branch at the

Who?	Does What?

Branch at the

National Level
State Level
Local Level

Who?	Does What?

Branch at the

National Level
State Level
Local Level

Who?	Does What?

Branch at the

National Level
State Level
Local Level

Representation in the House

Read the text, look at the map, and answer the questions.

The Senate is made up of 100 senators, or two senators per state. The House of Representatives is made up of 435 representatives. A state's population determines how many representatives it can have in the House of Representatives. States with more people have a greater number of representatives. Since 1790, the U.S. Constitution has required that a census (population count) of the states be taken every ten years to determine state representation in the House of Representatives.

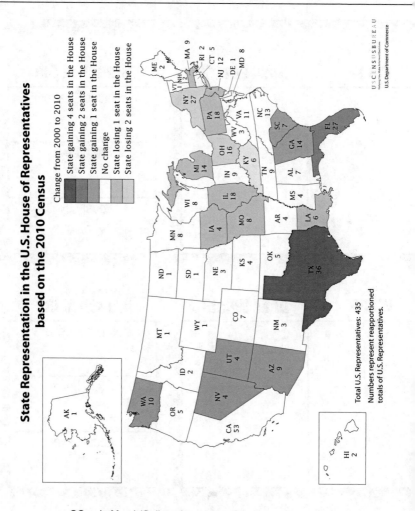

State Representation in the U.S. House of Representatives based on the 2010 Census

Change from 2000 to 2010

- State gaining 4 seats in the House
- State gaining 2 seats in the House
- State gaining 1 seat in the House
- No change
- State losing 1 seat in the House
- State losing 2 seats in the House

Total U.S. Representatives: 435
Numbers represent reapportioned totals of U.S. Representatives.

U.S. CENSUS BUREAU
U.S. Department of Commerce

1. A. Define census as it is used in the text.
   B. Explain why a census is required every ten years.

2. How are the Senate and House of Representatives different in regard to representation?

PART B: Use the U.S. House of Representatives apportionment map to answer the questions.

3. What is the purpose of the shading on the map?

4. Explain the purpose of the numbers on the map. What do you know about California from its number?

5. What can you determine about the state of Texas (TX)? What about New York (NY)? What about Colorado (CO)?

6. Do larger states typically have a larger population? Cite evidence from the map to support your conclusion.

7. Which states lost 2 or more seats in the House of Representatives? Which states gained 2 or more representatives in 2010?

8. Make inferences from the map to identify which areas of the country have experienced the highest rates of population growth.

9. In a well-organized essay, explain how state population determines state representation in the House of Representatives. Include a definition of representation and examples from the map to illustrate the effect of state population. Proofread and edit your work.

PART C: Individually or in small groups, create a poster to encourage people in your state to participate in the census. Use information from the text and map. Combine words and visuals to communicate your message. Display your poster for your class.

How a Bill Becomes a Law

A bill can be written by a citizen or any member of the House of Representatives or the Senate. This flowchart outlines the basic steps by which a bill passes through the House and Senate into law.

Look at the flowchart and answer the questions.

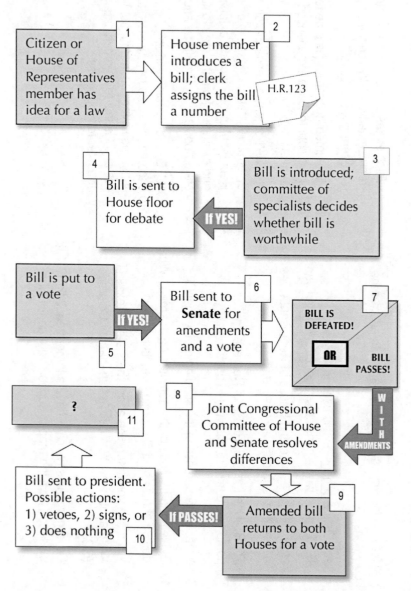

1. Citizen or House of Representatives member has idea for a law

2. House member introduces a bill; clerk assigns the bill a number — H.R.123

3. Bill is introduced; committee of specialists decides whether bill is worthwhile

4. **If YES!** Bill is sent to House floor for debate

5. Bill is put to a vote

6. **If YES!** Bill sent to **Senate** for amendments and a vote

7. BILL IS DEFEATED! **OR** BILL PASSES!

WITH AMENDMENTS

8. Joint Congressional Committee of House and Senate resolves differences

9. Amended bill returns to both Houses for a vote

10. **If PASSES!** Bill sent to president. Possible actions: 1) vetoes, 2) signs, or 3) does nothing

11. ?

PART A: Use the text and diagram to infer whether each statement is **true** or **false**.

. _____ A bill can be introduced only by a member of the House of Representatives.

. _____ Ordinary citizens cannot make suggestions for laws.

. _____ A bill must first be approved by the Senate before it can be sent to the House of Representatives.

. _____ A Joint Congressional Committee resolves differences between the Senate and House.

PART B: Using the flowchart, number the steps in order.

. _____ A bill is sent to the Senate and then to a committee for review.

. _____ The amended bill is returned to both Houses for a vote.

. _____ The bill is assigned a number.

. _____ A citizen or representative shares his or her idea for a bill.

. _____ A Joint Congressional Committee meets to resolve any differences between the original bill and the amended bill.

0. _____ Committee members decide whether the bill is worthwhile.

1. _____ The bill is sent to the president for approval.

PART C: Answer the following questions.

2. Explain the purpose of a committee of specialists.

3. What role does the president play in the passage of laws?

4. Use the flowchart to support the statement, "It is much more difficult to pass a bill than to kill it."

PART D: Use an online or classroom resource to answer the questions.

5. Research possible outcomes for step 11 based upon the president's action in step 10.

6. From original drafting to final law, how long is the typical life cycle of a bill?

Judicial Branch

Read the text and answer the questions.

The judicial branch of the United States government is outlined in Article III of the U.S. Constitution. The judicial branch contains the Supreme Court and the lower courts. Those lower courts include the 94 U.S. district courts, which try most federal cases, and the 13 U.S. courts of appeals, which handle appeals of district court cases. An appeal is a legal proceeding where a decision made by a lower court is brought before a higher court for review.

The judicial branch interprets the laws by deciding whether or not a law is allowed by our Constitution. As the highest court in the judicial branch, the Supreme Court does not actually try cases. It hears appeals from lower courts and decides whether or not their rulings are permitted under the Constitution.

The Supreme Court is made up of nine justices, including one chief justice and eight associate justices. These justices are appointed by the president and approved or rejected by the Senate. Justices serve for life unless impeached by Congress.

Supreme Court decisions are final. Many decisions have had far-reaching impacts on the United States. One example is the 1954 *Brown v. Board of Education* case that made racial segregation in schools illegal. Another important case is the *Miranda v. Arizona* case in 1966. This case required police to inform suspects of their rights.

1. Why is the Supreme Court considered the highest court in the judicial branch?

2. Where does the Supreme Court get its power to interpret the laws?

3. What checks do the president and the Congress have on the Supreme Court?

4. In small groups, use an online resource to research the who, what, when, and where of an influential Supreme Court decision. How did the case affect the law? Create a visual presentation and share with your class.

Federal Courts

ook at the chart and answer the questions.

Courts of the Federal Judicial Branch		
Examples	**#**	**Details**
U.S. Supreme Court	1	• 9 judges • most important court • located in Washington, D.C. • hears appeals from U.S. Circuit Courts of Appeals • may hear cases from state Supreme Courts in special cases • of about 10,000 petitions annually, hears less than 100 cases per year
U.S. Circuit Courts of Appeals	13	• 3 judges (usually) • hear appeals from district court cases • do not hear any new facts or look at evidence • check for legal mistakes made at previous district court trials
U.S. District Courts	94	• 2-28 judges each • every state has at least one court • federal cases begin here • hear civil and criminal cases • trial courts

. Which level of the federal courts conducts trials?

. What is the purpose of the U.S. Circuit Courts of Appeals?

. How do the three federal courts differ in the types of cases they hear?

. Why are there nearly 100 U.S. District Courts?

. Explain how a case first tried in the U.S. District Courts might eventually be heard by the Supreme Court.

. What can you infer about the Supreme Court by the small percentage of cases it hears?

Checks & Balances

The Constitution separates the government into three branches and assigns powers to each. Some of these powers are meant to keep the branches from abusing their power through a system of checks and balances.

Use information from the diagram to complete the cause and effect graphic organizer.

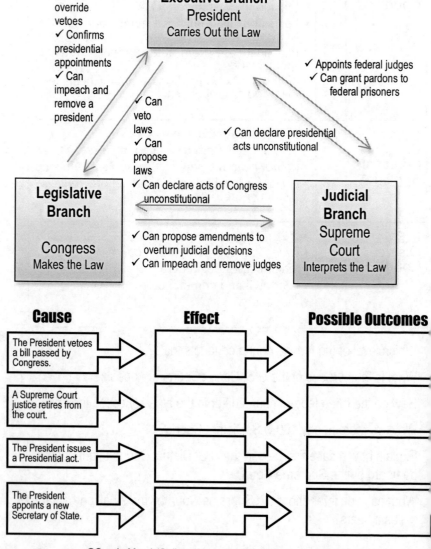

✓ Can override vetoes
✓ Confirms presidential appointments
✓ Can impeach and remove a president

Executive Branch
President
Carries Out the Law

✓ Appoints federal judges
✓ Can grant pardons to federal prisoners

✓ Can veto laws
✓ Can propose laws
✓ Can declare acts of Congress unconstitutional

✓ Can declare presidential acts unconstitutional

Legislative Branch

Congress
Makes the Law

✓ Can propose amendments to overturn judicial decisions
✓ Can impeach and remove judges

Judicial Branch
Supreme Court
Interprets the Law

Cause	Effect	Possible Outcomes
The President vetoes a bill passed by Congress.		
A Supreme Court justice retires from the court.		
The President issues a Presidential act.		
The President appoints a new Secretary of State.		

Appointing a Justice

This 1930 political cartoon depicts President Hoover trying to decide whom to nominate for Chief Justice of the U.S. Supreme Court after the Senate rejected his first choice.

Analyze the cartoon and answer the questions.

Courtesy of The National Archives

A. What branch of government is represented by arrow A?

B. What branch of government is represented by arrow B?

What power is A exercising? What power is B exercising?

What can you infer about B's opinion of A? Why?

What is the main message of this cartoon? What words or symbols helped you reach your conclusion?

What can you infer about the cartoonists' opinion of President Hoover? Cite details from the cartoon to support your answer.

Branches of Government

Complete the graphic organizer for each vocabulary word.

appeal

bicameral

Cabinet

checks and balances

compromise

delegate

executive branch

impeach

judicial branch

legislative branch

separation of powers

veto

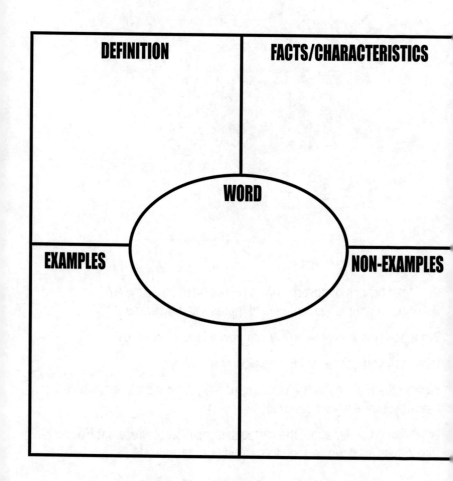